Franklin and Winston

A Christmas That Changed the World

Douglas Wood

illustrated by Barry Moser

CANDLEWICK PRESS

First edition 2011

Library of Congress Cataloging-in-Publication Data
Wood, Douglas, date.
Franklin and Winston : a Christmas that changed the world / Doug Wood. —1st ed.
p. cm.
Includes bibliographical references.
ISBN 978-0-7636-3383-7
1. World War, 1939–1945—Diplomatic history—Juvenile literature. 2. United States—Foreign
relations—Great Britain—Juvenile literature. 3. Great Britain—Foreign relations—United States—
Juvenile literature. 4. Roosevelt, Franklin D. (Franklin Delano), 1882–1945—Juvenile literature.
5. Churchill, Winston, Sir, 1874–1965—Juvenile literature. I. Title.

D753.W59 2010
940.53′2—dc22   2008025456
11 12 13 14 15 16 SWT 10 9 8 7 6 5 4 3 2 1

Printed in Dongguan, Guangdong, China

This book was typeset in Galliard.
The illustrations were done in watercolor.

Candlewick Press
99 Dover Street
Somerville, Massachusetts 02144

visit us at www.candlewick.com

✣ ✣ ✣

Winston Churchill and Franklin Roosevelt touched countless families in countless ways, large and small. To my dad and mother, my uncles and grandparents, and to all the families who shared and sacrificed through those vital years, I dedicate this book.

D. W.

The paintings illustrating this story are dedicated to Emily Crowe, my wife, my best friend for life.

B. M.

*I*T WAS THE WINTER OF 1941.

The valiant battleship HMS *Duke of York* struggled against the screaming winds and forty-foot waves of a mighty December gale. On board, Winston S. Churchill, prime minister of Great Britain, calmly chomped his ever-present cigar as he strolled the pitching decks. He was going to meet the president of the United States. He was going to spend Christmas at the White House. He would not be stopped by a mere storm. He would not be stopped by a hurricane.

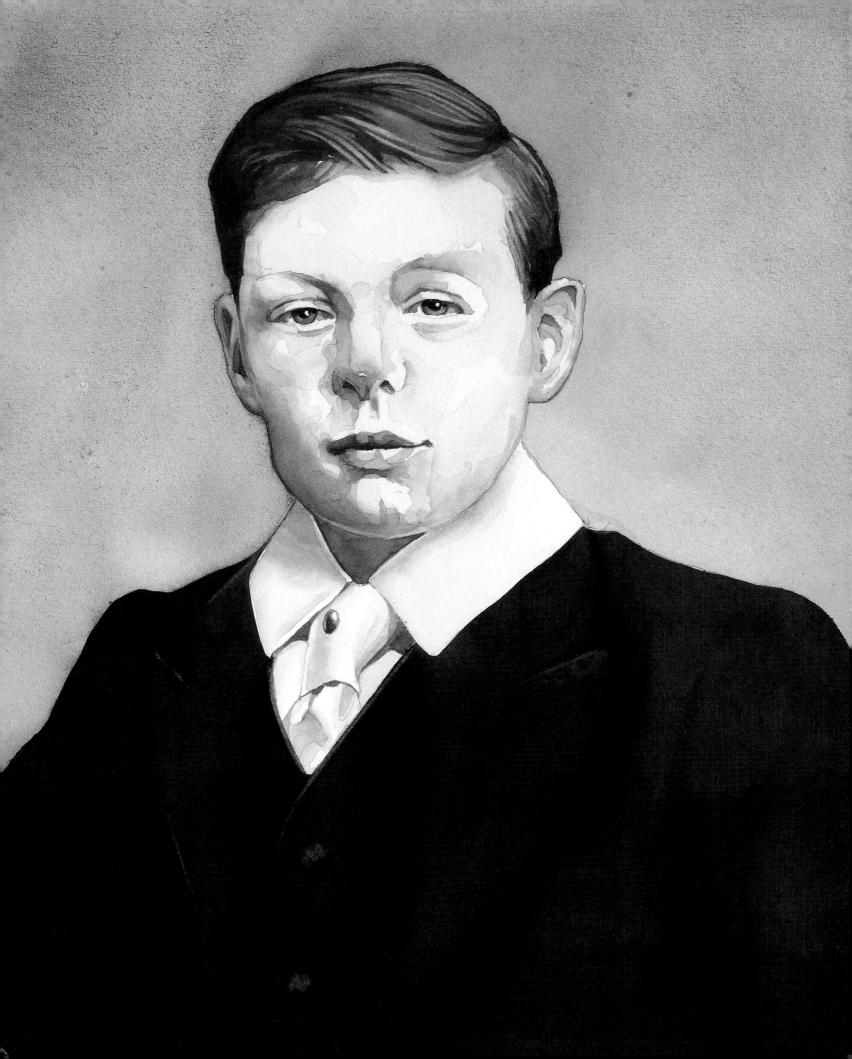

Since boyhood, Winston Churchill had dreamed of leading his proud island nation through historic times. But he had done poorly in school, and his father had told him he would never amount to anything.

Yet Winston had now led and inspired Great Britain through nearly two grim years of war. When asked to head the government, he had responded, "I have nothing to offer but blood, toil, tears, and sweat."

When Britain stood nearly alone against the terrible Nazi forces that swept across the globe, Winston had assured the British people: "We shall . . . ride out the storm of war. . . . We shall defend our island, whatever the cost may be. . . . We shall never surrender."

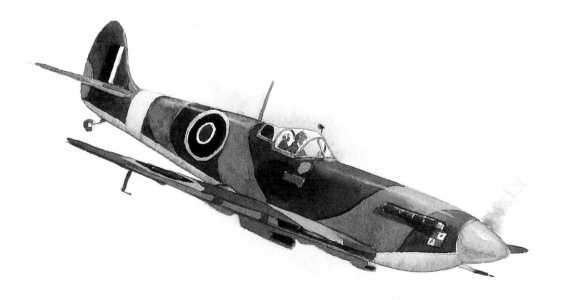

And when the Nazi Luftwaffe determined to bomb British cities to rubble, he had declared, "Let us . . . so bear ourselves that if the British Empire and its Commonwealth last for a thousand years, men will still say, 'This was their finest hour.'"

Even now, in this storm-tossed crossing, the prowling of Nazi submarines seemed more dangerous than the fury of the ocean. Yet Winston was his usual fearless, defiant self. His bulldog jaw jutted out. He was impatient to get over to the New World. Christmas was coming. He would spend it with the American president. And he and the president would plan how they might save the world.

In Washington, D.C., President Franklin Delano Roosevelt felt the weight of terrible events. Just a few days before, on December 7, 1941, the Japanese had launched a sneak attack on the U.S. naval base at Pearl Harbor, in Hawaii. Thousands were killed and much of the American fleet destroyed. After years of supporting Britain and other free nations, yet trying to remain somehow apart from the awful battles raging around the world, America was now at war.

All his life, since boyhood, Franklin Roosevelt had felt that he was destined for great things, to lift up his people and his country. Even after polio robbed him of the use of his legs, his buoyant spirit would not be conquered. Now, after guiding the nation through the desperate years of the Great Depression, after inspiring and encouraging millions, further greatness was required.

During the worst of the Depression, Franklin had assured Americans: "This great nation will endure as it has endured, will revive and will prosper. . . . The only thing we have to fear is fear itself."

After Pearl Harbor, he had declared: "We are now in the midst of a war, not for conquest, not for vengeance, but for a world in which this nation and all that this nation represents will be safe for our children."

And in a message to Winston Churchill, he had remarked, "We are all in the same boat now."

Now Franklin awaited the arrival of Winston's ship. Christmas was coming. He would spend it with the British prime minister. Together they would decide how to confront a menace that threatened all of civilization.

They had met twice before, these two leaders, and found that they got on well. In the past two years, they had corresponded many times by telephone and telegraph. But this would be their first chance to really get to know each other, and they were anxious to get started.

On December 22, when Winston finally reached America's Chesapeake Bay, he was too impatient to linger a minute longer. Further travel by boat or train or automobile would simply be too slow, and he could not stand the wait. So earlier plans were changed, and the prime minister and his closest aides were taken by plane up the Potomac River to Washington, D.C. They were thrilled by what they saw below — a sea of lights, whole cities lit up. Because of the constant threat of Nazi bombs, Britain's own cities had been under blackout for years.

As his plane touched down and the door opened, Churchill saw a tall man leaning against a long limousine. It was Roosevelt. Churchill had cabled the president not to trouble himself to meet the plane. But there he was. Winston hurried over to shake hands. They made an odd-looking pair, the short, stocky prime minister and the tall, elegant president.

Because of his polio, Franklin had to spend most of his time in a wheelchair. But on important occasions, he liked to stand on his own. He faced his disability with the same courage with which he faced all other challenges, the same courage he shared with the nation.

The limo whisked the two away to the White House, where an evening of celebration awaited them. Flashbulbs popped. Cameras clicked. Franklin jokingly mixed special drinks, and Winston, his eyes twinkling, made the rounds of all the guests, greeting each one, "How-de-do, how-de-do."

Dinner, hosted by Mrs. Roosevelt, was filled with light-hearted teasing and banter, and it ended with a toast by the president: "It has been in my head and in my heart now for a long time; now it is on the tip of my tongue: To the common cause!"

Then, at the end of an already long day, it was time for serious matters. Winston and his aides were led by the president to the Oval Room. Bookcases and models of ships lined the walls. There the men pored over maps and reports from around the world — Europe, the Mediterranean, Africa, Asia, the South Pacific. Everywhere there were threats and challenges, battles under way, decisions to be made, plans to be laid.

At midnight the meeting came to a close. But Winston had to take a sleeping pill. He was simply too excited to sleep.

The next day was busy, but the prime minister loved gardening and found the time to explore the White House grounds and gardens. He made a strange sight — bald-headed, dressed in his one-piece coveralls, puffing on a cigar.

By late afternoon, he had changed into more formal attire. It was time for his first American press conference. Reporters packed the room as Winston sat beside Franklin behind a crowded desk. "I wish you would stand up and let them see you," said the president. "They can't see you."

Winston happily obliged, climbing up on his chair and waving his cigar. The press loved it. And the president beamed, delighted with his friend's ability to win over an audience, just as he had so often done himself.

One after another, questions about the war and this new alliance were flung at the British leader. He answered them all with ease and humor. But one question stumped him. "Mr. Minister, when do you think we'll lick these boys?"

Winston looked puzzled. An aide hurried over and translated the American expression. The prime minister smiled. "If we manage it well," he answered, "it will only take half as long as if we manage it badly."

The room rocked with laughter.

The Roosevelts and their White House staff soon found that Winston could be a difficult houseguest. No one had ever seen anyone quite like him before. Not feeling comfortable in the room that Eleanor Roosevelt had chosen for him, he chose another. There was to be no talking or whistling in the halls outside his room, he insisted. And he would need two hot baths a day.

He stayed up till all hours of the night, smoking cigars and wandering the White House halls in his nightgown. And he often kept the president up far later than Eleanor thought he should. The "Winston hours," they were called. But the president didn't seem to mind. Winston, he said, made life in the White House more fun.

Both men preferred to get up late in the morning, having breakfast and doing much of their morning work in bed. They would often drop into each other's rooms unannounced when they had something important to discuss. One day Franklin barged into Winston's room just as he was getting out of the tub. "Think nothing of it," said Winston. "The prime minister of Great Britain has nothing to conceal from the president of the United States!"

Meanwhile, the days and nights were packed with important meetings and difficult negotiations — even arguments. The two leaders had so much to discuss, so many decisions to make. All the details of fighting a great World War and creating the largest alliance in history had to be hammered out.

Generals, cabinet secretaries, and chiefs of staff met around the clock. Rooms were crowded with maps, telephones, and telegraphs to keep track of events around the world. Most of the news was not good. Everywhere, it seemed, tyranny was advancing, freedom retreating. The two leaders keenly felt that the future of their countries and the world depended upon their decisions and on their ability to work together.

But they also saved room for a lighter side, for the strengthening bonds of friendship. Winston liked to wheel Franklin around in his wheelchair. They referred to each other by their first names. Both men loved to laugh and tell stories. And they were fond of ribbing and teasing.

Sometimes a barb would cut a bit deep. "Now, look here, Winston!" Franklin would protest. Winston would growl and chew his cigar.

And of course, there was Christmas to attend to as well, and all the matters of daily life in the White House. It was a house that had become, thanks to Eleanor and Franklin, a beacon of hope for millions of other homes and families in difficult times.

On Christmas Eve, the time came to light the National Christmas Tree, and Winston joined Franklin for the occasion. A great crowd had gathered on the lawn, and the warm and comforting sounds of carols drifted on the cold night air. The president spoke: "Our strongest weapon in this war is . . . the dignity and brotherhood of man which Christmas Day signifies — more than any other day or any other symbol."

Then he introduced Churchill, "My associate, my old and good friend." Winston, shivering from the cold, stepped to the microphone. "I spend this anniversary and festival far from my country, far from my family, yet I cannot truthfully say that I feel far from home. . . . We may cast aside, for this night at least, the cares and dangers which beset us, and make for the children an evening of happiness in a world of storm. . . . Let the children have their night of fun and laughter. Let the gifts of Father Christmas delight their play. . . . In God's mercy, a happy Christmas to you all."

On Christmas morning, Franklin invited Winston to join his family for a service and hymns at Foundry Methodist Church. For a short time, the prime minister was able to forget the horrors of war and all his burdens. "I'm glad I went," he said. "It's the first time my mind has been at rest in a long time."

Christmas night brought a grand dinner, hosted by Eleanor. Dozens of Roosevelt friends and family mingled with their  British guests. It was a magnificent setting, and Franklin proudly carved the turkey. The conversation was lively, but Winston was unusually quiet and excused himself early. Tomorrow he would give one of the most important speeches of his life. He would address the Congress of the United States of America.

Long into the night he worked on his thoughts. He knew that many in Congress were recently opposed to alliance with Britain in the war. He might not get a warm reception from what he called the "Parliament of the Great Republic."

The next day, as Winston boarded the motorcade to Capitol Hill, Franklin Roosevelt warmly wished his friend good luck. But Winston didn't need it. He was one of the greatest speakers of the English language, and he was ready for the moment.

As he stood in the historic chamber, his words rang with vigor and confidence. The congressmen cheered and stomped their feet. He made them laugh. He touched their hearts. He filled them with courage for the great conflict ahead. He growled like an English bulldog. When he had finished, the audience rose as one. And when he flashed his famous V-for-victory sign, their cheers became a roar.

Listening on the radio back at the White House, just as millions of other Americans listened, Franklin knew that his friend had triumphed. The alliance would go forward. Through the long and difficult years ahead, their two countries would fight as one. Victory would be achieved.

New Year's Day arrived, and with it an important ceremony. Most of the main ideas of the Grand Alliance had been agreed to, and it was time to announce their new partnership to the world. Franklin had fretted for days about exactly what to call the agreement and had finally settled on "The Declaration of the United Nations." Winston happily concurred. Even Fala, Franklin's beloved Scottish terrier, looked pleased.

The two leaders and representatives from other countries agreed to work and fight together to defeat the Axis Powers, which sought to enslave the world. They agreed "to defend life, liberty, independence, and religious freedom, and to preserve human rights and justice in their own lands as well as in other lands."

Afterward, Winston autographed one of his books for Franklin: *Inscribed for President Franklin D. Roosevelt by Winston S. Churchill. In rough times, January 1942.*

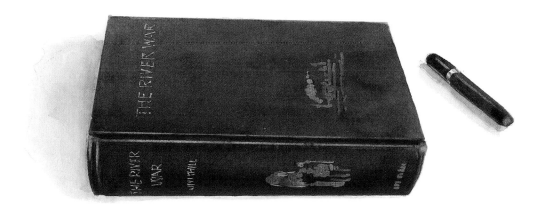

When the last of their meetings were over and it was time for Winston to return home, the two friends had a final dinner with the president's top aide, Harry Hopkins. Warm sentiments were shared. Hopkins slipped Churchill a brief letter to take to Churchill's beloved wife, Clementine, back in Britain. *You would have been ever so proud of your husband*, Hopkins had written. *First because he was ever so good-natured. I didn't see him take anybody's head off. . . . If he had half as good a time here as the president did . . . he will surely carry pleasant memories.*

To his friend Winston Churchill, President Franklin Roosevelt simply said, "Trust me to the bitter end."

The two friends did trust each other, through every hardship and difficulty, victory and defeat, over the next four years of World War II. Millions of others trusted them as well, all around the world. It was a world they helped to save with their courage and their friendship, on that important

Christmas of 1941.

AFTERWORD

During their historic Christmas 1941 meetings, Winston Churchill and Franklin Roosevelt:

— established the greatest military alliance in history;

— crafted a charter for the United Nations;

— appointed the commanders of land, sea, and air forces;

—created the Combined Chiefs of Staff;

— set in motion the expansion of American industry to produce massive new quantities of munitions and war matériel;

— put in place the plans that would liberate more than thirty countries and hundreds of millions of people and eventually win World War II.

AUTHOR'S NOTE

My father, Jim, served in Italy and Arabia during World War II. His brother, my uncle Dick, parachuted behind enemy lines on D-day and was killed at the terrible Battle of the Bulge. On my mother's side of the family, my uncle Wilbur fought across North Africa, Sicily, and up the Italian peninsula, including at Anzio and Cassino, and my uncle Bob served in the U.S. Navy. My maternal granddad and grandmother kept extensive scrapbooks and news clippings from every day of the great war as they waited for their son to return. We still have those scrapbooks.

Like many of my generation, I heard all my life of those momentous times and of the two great men to whom the world turned for inspiration and leadership.

BIBLIOGRAPHY

Alter, Jonathan. *The Defining Moment: FDR's Hundred Days and the Triumph of Hope*. New York: Simon & Schuster, 2006.

Ambrose, Stephen E., and C. L. Sulzberger. *New History of World War II*. New York: Viking, 1997.

Bercuson, David, and Holger Herwig. *One Christmas in Washington*. New York: Overlook Press, 2005.

Churchill, Winston S. *Blood, Toil, Tears, and Sweat: The Speeches of Winston Churchill*. Edited by David Cannadine. Boston: Houghton Mifflin, 1989.

——. *The Second World War, Volume 1: The Gathering Storm*. Boston: Houghton Mifflin, 1948.

——. *The Second World War, Volume 2: Their Finest Hour*. Boston: Houghton Mifflin, 1949.

——. *The Second World War, Volume 3: The Grand Alliance*. Boston: Houghton Mifflin, 1950.

Country Beautiful editors. *A Man of Destiny: Winston S. Churchill*. Waukesha, WI: Country Beautiful Foundation, 1965.

Golway, Terry. *Together We Cannot Fail: FDR and the American Presidency*. Naperville, IL: Sourcebooks, 2009.

Keegan, John. *The Second World War*. New York: Penguin, 1989.

Loewenheim, Francis L., Harold D. Langley, and Manfred Jonas. *Roosevelt and Churchill: Their Secret Wartime Correspondence*. New York: Saturday Review Press, 1975.

Meacham, Jon. *Franklin and Winston: An Intimate Portrait of an Epic Friendship*. New York: Random House, 2003.

Newspapers of the day from the collection of *D. W. Wilton*.